CANADIAN DENTAL APTITUDE TEST (DAT)

SOAP CARVING

PRACTICE PROBLEM SERIES

Canadian Dental Aptitude Test (DAT)

Soap Carving
Practice Problem Series 5

Oscar Willis

This book is dedicated to the reader and all dental school applicants for the dedication in pursuing a life to better the health of humanity.

Table of Contents

Introduction

The Canadian DAT is unique from the American DAT and amongst other professional graduate entrance exams in that there is a manual dexterity test component. The Canadian DAT is acceptable in Canada and the United States but not vice versa, hence there is motivation for writing a single exam that is accepted in North America. The carving section of the Canadian DAT requires a certain amount of manual dexterity that can be developed through practice.

The carving section is the first component of the DAT and the applicant is given 30 minutes to carve the soap. There is 5 minutes at the beginning provided to inspect the soap and the soap carving diagram. Materials include soap, knife handle, knife blade, Sharpie marker, pencil, flexible ruler, and soap carving diagram.

Practice Problems

All measurements are in millimeters (not necessarily drawn to scale).

Directions for Carving:

The illustrations near the top show how the carving should appear when it is completed.

The carving exercise consists of 3 parts (2 ends and 1 surface pattern). It is important that all 3 parts be completed to be considered for high scoring.

You may use the small ridge on the top and bottom as midlines for carving relationships.

The dimensions should be followed as closely as possible. The carving will be evaluated on accurate and complete reproduction of the pattern in measurements and design, smoothness and flatness of planes, sharpness of angles, symmetry and orientation of the 3 parts.

DIRECTIONS FOR HANDING IN THE CARVING:

1. Print your name, identification number and test centre code on an uncut surface of your carving and also on the napkin.

2. Wrap your carving carefully and securely so that it may be shipped safely for grading. Fold the napkin in such a way that the carving will not fall out.

3. Hand in your wrapped carving to your evaluation proctor.

    Shaded area denotes cut surface.

    *This dimension can vary depending on the overall length of the carving.

Carving Design #1

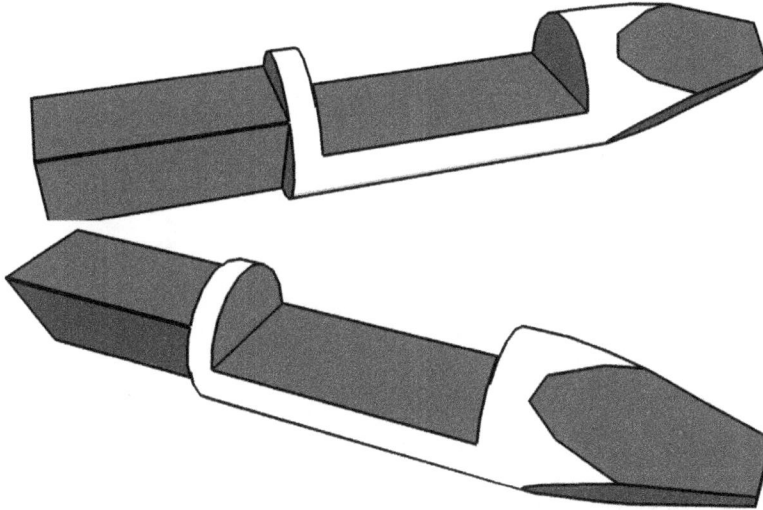

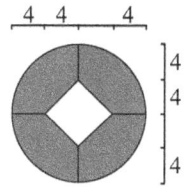

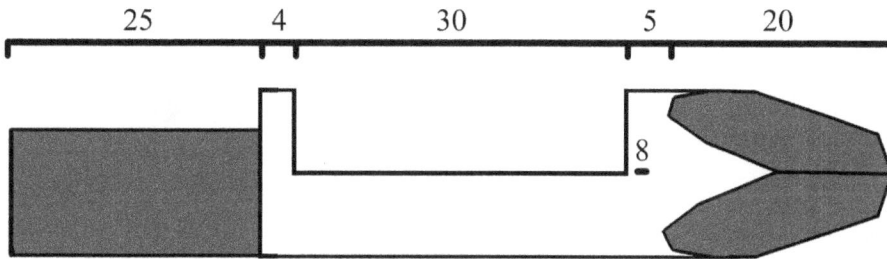

Side View

Top View

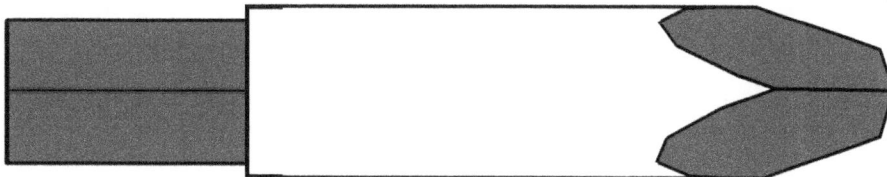

Bottom View

Carving Design #2

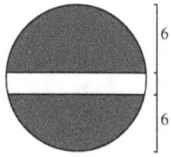

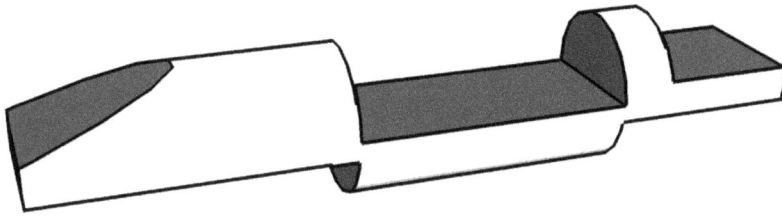

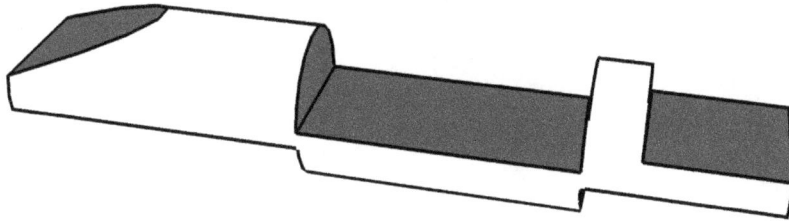

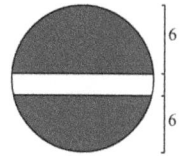

15	18	30	15

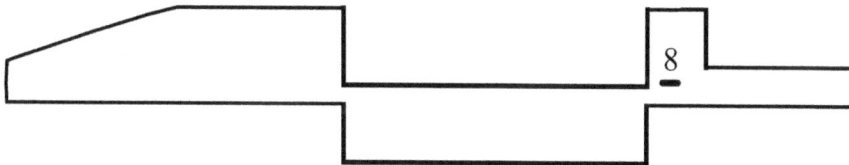

Side View

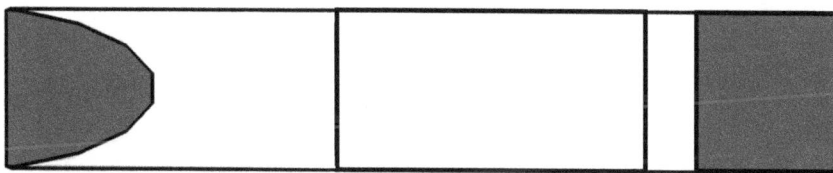

Top View

Bottom View

10

Carving Design #3

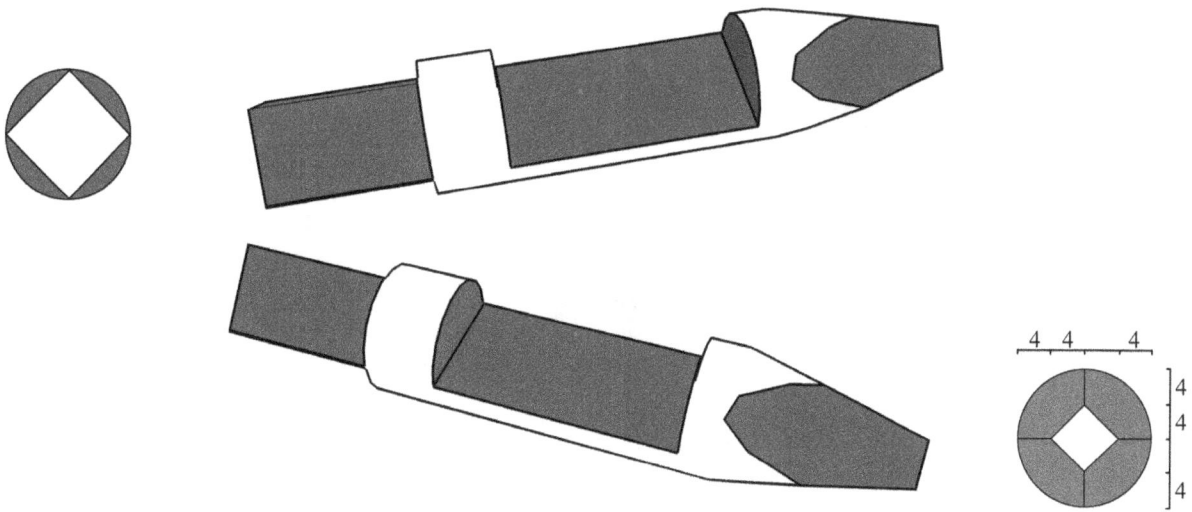

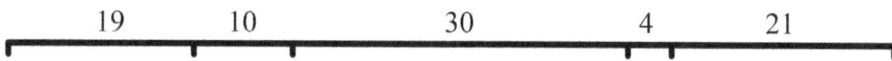

Side View

Top View

Bottom View

Carving Design #4

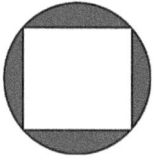

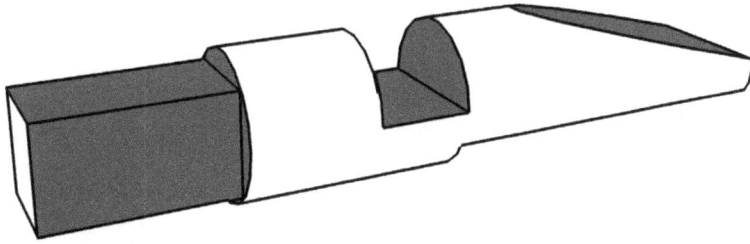

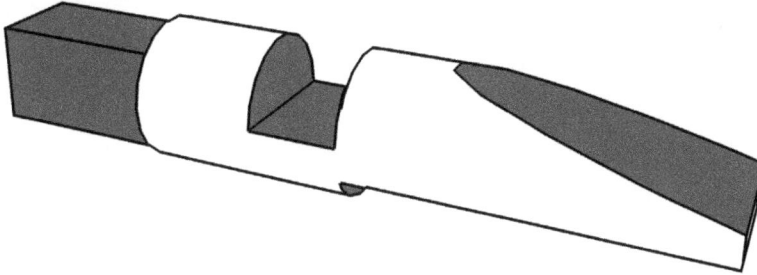

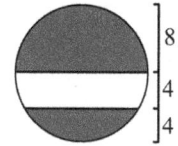

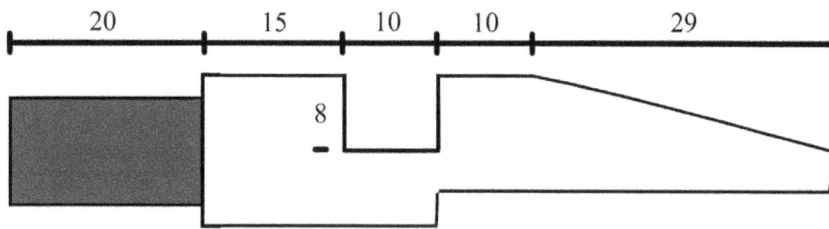

Side View

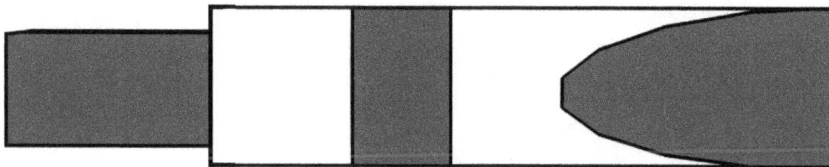

Top View

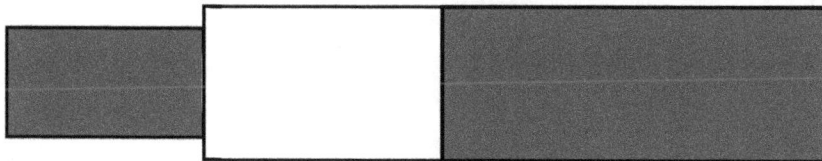

Bottom View

14

Carving Design #5

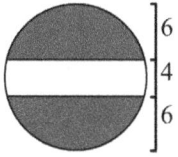

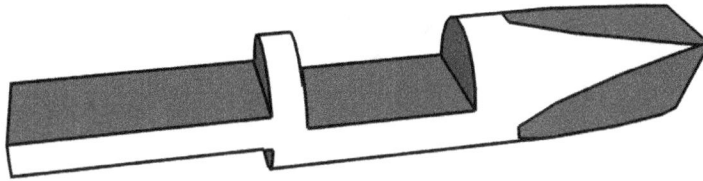

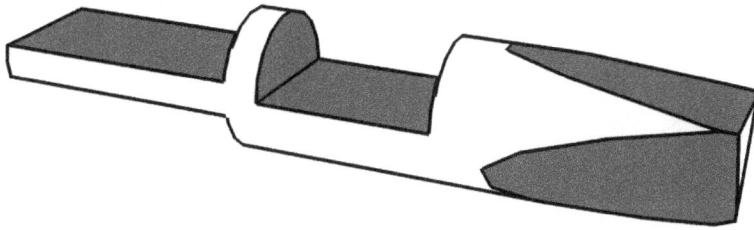

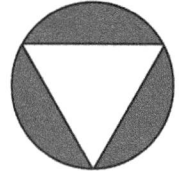

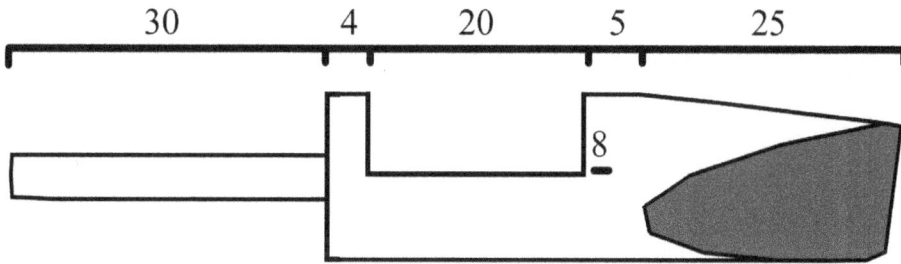

Side View

Top View

Bottom View

More practice available with the:

Canadian Dental Aptitude Test (DAT)

Soap Carving

Practice Problem Series
1-5